Disimprison

Disimprison

✦

Freeing My Soul; Speaking My Heart

Syieve Locklair

Author of Sayings of a Soul

iUniverse, Inc.
New York Bloomington Shanghai

Disimprison
Freeing My Soul; Speaking My Heart

iUniverse books may be ordered through booksellers or by contacting:

iUniverse
1663 Liberty Drive
Bloomington, IN 47403
www.iuniverse.com
1-800-Authors (1-800-288-4677)

Because of the dynamic nature of the Internet, any Web addresses or links contained in this book may have changed since publication and may no longer be valid.

The views expressed in this work are solely those of the author and do not necessarily reflect the views of the publisher, and the publisher hereby disclaims any responsibility for them.

ISBN: 978-0-595-52148-7 (pbk)
ISBN: 978-0-595-62212-2 (ebk)

Printed in the United States of America

For Mama & Daddy, with everlasting love

For those who are REAL

For those who are TRUE

And ...

*For those who are
"doing the damn thing"*

Contents

Acknowledgements
& Shout-outs

The One who bestowed upon me a talent that allows me to express myself and to share it with others.

My Family: Mama, Daddy, Tanya D., Jen-Jen, Kim, Sonja, Pat, Lamont, Nana, Ty, my uncles, and my cousins—you are My All.

My Guardian Diva: Whitney Houston—
You will forever be "MY DIVA"—the 'Diva Originale.' I luv ya, Much!!

My Angels; My Rocks: Deidre Brown & Quiana Parler—For good times and bad times; you make them the best of times. Shyla, Chamberlin, Aaliyah … you are our future!

Those who inspire and support me & those who have touched my life in a special way: Natalia Brooker, Kim "Bama/Papa J." Johnson, Patrice Buckner, Mimi Badger, Leslie Marsh, Mike Moran, Jennifer Washington, Nikki Brown, Trina Wright, Josetta Brown-Wilkes, Shawanda Daniels, Jerolyn Murray, Shomoneik Grant, Brandi Williamson, Natalie Smith, Tammy Davis, Amanda Wiseley-Morisseau, Ms. Denise "Stuff" Dobson, Mrs. Shirley Johnson, Ms. Cassandra "Ms. B." Bolden, The Carvolhos (Diana, Diamond, & Sophie), Dentresa Thompson, LeConte C. Richardson (Luvs Ya, Porgy!), Paulette Vanderhorst, Mrs. Willette Burnham, Mwende "GG" Kiambo, Carolyn Robinson, Connie "B.O." Carroll, Bernadine Walden, Keith Davis, Meg Reinhardt, Wendy Calvin, Matt Walker, Bobby Taylor, Mary Ann Rivers, Samuella Holmes & Costella Green (I love you two, madly), Jezula "Ghetto Chik Boondisha" Antoine ("My Land"), Dennay Riley, Aisha Duncan, Sarah Yuen, Denise Epstein, Lauren "Big Sister Gorgeous One" Su, Tiffani Webb (my co-host!), Emily "Madame Emm" Martin, Lacy DeVeny (I want to be you when I grow up), Tonya Mackey, Planter (Denise … if you're nasty), Susan "Tomi" Berry (thanks for giving me 7 more habits), and first [if read backwards]—Jamell Lessington (ok, it took a while, but better late than …).

Special Friends: The RAWSISTAZ Reviewers, and Delores Thornton along with Blackrefer.com.

Family, Friends, and Fans who have supported me throughout this journey; I thank you deeply—you are a big part of me.

Now, if you feel I may have ~~intentionally~~ accidentally omitted you: Please charge it to my heart and not my head ... and vice versa! :) Nevertheless, this one's for you: _____, I thank you ... much!

I bow out!

This is a note. This is *only* a note! ☺

Okay, so it's <u>another</u> note.

You know I had to say, "THANK YOU!" 'Thank you for loving me; thank you for supporting me; thank you for taking the time to read the material I've worked to create.' You have great taste! I hope you like it.

As you may already know, much of my work is "inspired in part by" some significant motivational force in my life (i.e., family, friends, love [and the pursuit of], relationships [or things similar in nature], opinions and outlooks on EVERY-THING, and the many aspects of life that shape us all into our individual, wonderful selves).

Disimprison: Freeing My Soul; Speaking My Heart talks of being in a "good place" when it looks as if you're in a "bad place." For every loss there is a gain; *Disimprison* seeks to show that being in a "bad" place can be positive; especially if you take something enlightening away from the experience. This is the point where you start fresh … start new … head yourself in the direction to get what you want, need, and deserve. Now is the time for you to do you. So, go ahead: be you … accept you … embrace you. Love you—the *new* you. I dare you.

Feel free to share your comments or feelings with me, say hello, or get my address to send me money and gifts: <u>SayingsOfASoul@yahoo.com</u> ☺ If I don't write you, I'll write you!

All the Best That I Can Give!

-Syieve

As I define it …
Disimprison—*to openly express oneself and and permit one's soul to accept and experience the happier and positive aspects of life.*
Will you define it likewise?

DISIMPRISON

It's time to break free
Unleash the inner, the outer; the all of me
Take the world by storm
No more of the unusual; prepare to see The Norm
This is where I free my soul
Release testimonies that should've been long told
This is where I speak my heart
Dishing everything; filtering no part
Brace yourself
Be ready
Judgment Day is near;
The deliverance of a new me is already here
No longer bound to other's wants and expectations
From this point I rise to higher elevations
Eager to accept the joys and opportunities that have arisen
This is my time to DISIMPRISON

Are you ready for it?

RESCUING ME

Spreading my wings before I fly
Embracing my future; never another lie
Breaking away; unlocking the chain
Cleansing myself of the self-inflicted pain
Resuscitating my soul; giving it life, removing the dead
Speaking the words I should have said
Doing now what I should have done then
Finding … accepting … being in the truth
I vow to live my life; starting here without an end
This is my testimony; prepare for the proof

No more bottling, trapping, and holding things inside
I'm letting it flow
Like it or love it; I'm showing my pride
No more feeling like I'm bound, gagged, and tied
I'm letting everyone know
Take it or leave it; I'm refusing to hide

Raising myself to a new elevation
Standing in the light, becoming my own salvation
Hearing truths I never told
The ones I thought would never be spoken
Like how *we* didn't love me
But, that was then …
And this is the way it's going to be
A reclamation of my soul
And a celebration of the new me

WHATCHA SEE

Whatcha see is whatcha see
Whatcha see is whatcha crave
Whatcha see is whatcha feel
Whatcha see is whatcha want
Whatcha see is whatcha need
Whatcha see is *all* ya get
Whatcha see is me.

IT'S HARD BEING BEAUTIFUL

Do I make you drool?
     Do I make you sweat?
When I walk into a room, why do you lose your cool and get all wet?

Every place I go;
     Everything I wear;
          Everyone I talk to—
I feel your stare.

You gossip about things I did, when *I* wasn't even there

What's so intriguing about my life,
     It makes you want to care?

Don't photo my actions; Don't copy my walk
I never intended to turn you on or make you want to stalk

Stop following me around and quit minding my business.
     You're so lame.
I do what you do; You do what I do.
     Baby, we are all the same.

I'm tired;
     So I turn my back, mine my bid'ness, and try to walk away.
But you;
     You're clueless; don't get the hint; you lie; you push and you pull.

Living life is easy, but damn it is *hard* being beautiful.

ONE SIMPLE PLAN

This life is mine to follow the plan:
            One life
                  One love
                        One man
You think it's easy, but it's not;
      Living day to day; always giving good lovin',
      When gettin' "no love" is *all* you've got

You can lose your mind,
      Trying to find a partner for life's simple plan:
            One life
                  One love
                        One man
In a crowd, I sit and stare;
      My body's there,
      but my mind is everywhere.

Everyone says, "he's alright,"
      But they don't know I'm sad and empty—
            My soul is cold; I have no one to
            hold—
            And can't sleep at night.

      … it's so amusing, but it's so damn confusing …

Even with the strife, this is my only life;
      And I have to live it live all for me—
            Set my mind and body free.
      Be true to myself;
            Don't lie to me or anybody.

It's confusing to see things differently while trying to understand the mystery of this plan:
      One life, One love, One man.

But, it's amazing to see how hard it is to be happy when all I really need is to be hugged and l.o.v.e.d.

One man.   One love.   One life.

LIONIZE!

I came into your life to quench your thirst
But before you taste the nectar,
There are some rules we must establish first:
Since you have chosen to accept this mission
   Don't speak to me unless
   I have given permission
Thou shalt not touch thee, for thou shall be burned
   My body is a treasure
   A reward, which must be earned
I demand better than the rest
   That's just who I am
   I don't do less
My sexiness is tempting, but don't stare
   I know you desire me and want to be like me
   But I, really, don't care
It's my way or the highway
   There's no other way; no halfway, no tomorrow.
   Just all the way—today!

Since *This* is said and *That* is understood,
  we can begin.
Just remember that I am the legend.

I am:
   The sun, the moon, the air, and the sky.
   The writer, producer, director, and the star.

     The Legend. The Leo!

As a reminder:
   If I don't say it with my chords, I'll say it with my eyes …

     You better, Lionize!

PERSEVERANCE

You can knock me down, but I'll get back up;
    never stop
Gon' keep on fightin' and survivin' 'til I reach the top
Getting wiser and stronger; lastin' beyond the point
    where I beat you
Standin' tall with pride—
    Up and over you—
    Holding down spots #'s 1 and 2
I'm gonna keep on doing what it is I do
And that includes, baby, defeating you

CONTAGIOUS: THE DIAGNOSIS

You're a sickness that keeps pulling me back into the same old mess
I'm going to get over you—
      that's for sure
            … so I'm not gon stress …
Keep searching and fighting—
      'Til I find a cure
You're bad for my health
I've never had a problem getting over anyone else

CONTAGIOUS: THE DISEASE

From looking in your eyes the night we met
I should've known then this friendship I would regret
How could I have prevented myself from falling?
Falling for someone whose voice had my heart reaching out and calling
Just from the intense attention you gave
I knew you were someone I would desire, feen, and enthusiastically crave

As much as I wanted to belong ... I should've known we had to go wrong

The very first time you lied
I delivered tears like I've never cried
I should've ended it then and called it a loss
Instead of enduring the pain, tests, and emotional costs

I burn with fever the moment we touch
I become weak the instant you speak
Mama never told me love would hurt so much

Hurts me so, cause you won't let go
If only you could be mi amore, I wouldn't run towards the door

You're so contagious you infect me internally
You hurt me so much, but I want you here—whispering tenderly in my ear;
Massaging gently my entire body—
Relieving me of the pain ... reliving your love, again

I starve you like a fever; feed you like a cold
Give you all the remedies I've ever been told
I run 'til I sweat; medicate; even your sheets I burn
Just when I think I'm better, I get weak, and you return

I try to improve my immune deficiency,
But it's when I'm physically stronger and emotionally spent that you attack me

The pain you bring tortures endlessly
I need you to go away, but also want you to stay
But how can this be; given the way you treat me

You persistently return to ruin my health
I allow it to happen, so I can only blame myself

How could one person be so unhealthy for me …
Emotionally? Physically? Mentally? Socially? Spiritually?

Who would have thought:
     A Love so outrageous and so contagious
         And so loving …
     Could be so unhealthy and so dangerous

CONTAGIOUS: THE RECOVERY

The storm is over now;
    The sun is out;
        The sky is blue
The Fat Lady's sung;
    This war is won;
        And I'm finally over you.

LAST TIME

I'm tired of hanging my heart out on the line
Only for you to return, thinking everything is fine

Hand-washed; machine-washed; steamed; and dry-cleaned;
    Even bleach can't remove the traces of your dirt
I've come to know, first-hand and face-to-face, the outcome of your actions—
    The pain; the hurt

A tear that's cried, a mirror that's shattered, a heart that's bled
All results of a new path where your feet have tread;
    The place where they and the ground have wed

Leave your key lying next to me,
    The next time your mind or heart leads you to roam
For our house will no longer be your home

I guess this heart of mine will have to be demolished and garbaged
Cause I can't give someone something you've used and damaged

GHETTO LOVE: LIKE WHITNEY LOVES BOBBY (OR LOVED)

Our love is lean and mean; you and me. We are loveable fitness.
Be down with me. In a case of court, b.a.b.y. be my witness
When I wake each morning, it's your praises that I sing
(Pride, Joy, & Respect) You are the only air lifting my wing

SPECIAL KIND OF LOVE

Sitting at the kitchen table,
    Admiring that perfect red rose
Ever since I was a little child,
    I've longed to receive one of those

Mesmerized by its beauty as it absorbs the water in its vase
But can't seem to look pass the reflection of the sullen expression on my face

I never thought I would be sharing in this kind of love;
    In this kind of way
Though I'm thinking about the gift I'm going to give to myself next Valentine's
Day

I've always imagined someone giving me these gifts I've received
Cause I've never dreamt of accepting this love in which I've never believed

A red rose, chocolate kisses, caramel chews, and candle light
    This is ideal.
I've finally made it to the day, where my moment is real

Always envisioned being this happy by relying on someone else
But I've found this love and given this love in gifts—
    All of, to, and from myself

HOW I SEE IT

I have to close my eyes and lock my heart; just to get some rest
I need time to prepare my soul and brace myself, so I can return with my very
best

I'm so tired; I'm so strained. My energy's long been drained
All the tears and fighting show 'nothing' is all I've gained

I choose and I refuse to pick another door when I always lose

It's the pain and the food that causes me to get fatter
While I turn around and walk alone over the broken glass that has shattered
People stare at me and I stare at them; we all pretend like nothing's the matter

But I'm tired of all this.... My opportunities should be knockin'
By this time next year, I want my life to be rockin'

How I feel, I can't accurately describe—
        Though I've tried and I've tried. Oh, how I've tried.
It's been so long, I feel numb; I feel dumb.
        I think a part of me has died.

I don't know how much more of this I can take
When the only thing I can count on is having a heartache

My body is weak; no one will be around
My emotions are burned,
To be safe and protect myself, all I can do is
        Shut them down.

WITH ARMS WIDE OPEN

My bed is cold
My arms are empty
My heart aches
My fear … this is my fate

I'm the scarecrow in the field with his arms stretched wide
Eagerly waiting for company to parch at his side

There's always The Guy that passes me by
And makes me wonder why it is not I
He wants to give a try

Can he not see that I'm sad and lonely
And want him to have and hold me
Share the chance to love each other; unconditionally

I desire to love Him like He will love me
Though my open availability may be causing his hesitancy
I will love him like we'll forever last
But I grow jaded after another lost day has passed
I lower my head and look around me at the untroddened dirt
And still long to love like it's never going to hurt

A representation of my feelings is what this is suppose to be
Therefore, I end it as a replica of how I feel:
                    i-n-c-o-m-p-l-e-t-e

I'M THE ONE YOU WERE BORN TO SEEK

I'm the last piece to your puzzle until it's solved
I'm the one with whom you want to connect with and be involved

I'm the one who loves more than what I could ever give
I'm the one who fills your soul and heart with the desire to live

I'm the spirit that gave your broken heart the strength to mend
I'm the lover with whom the rest of your life you will spend

I'm the air you breathe
I'm the thoughts you think
I'm the flavors you savor and the words you speak
I'm the one who inspired this immaculate hunt
I am the one *you* were born to seek

DISCOMBOBULATED: THE BLAME GAME

It is you I couldn't keep from loving if I tried
It is you whom I must slam the door on from where it was once opened wide
And so it is you whose eyes I must look into and say this dreadful good-bye

It is you who make me smile with the words of your speech
It is you my heart wants when your body isn't within reach

It is you who the thought of drives me crazy
It is you who knows exactly how to hold me
And it is you who I need to set my heart free

It is you who holds the match I fear will burn
It is you who will never love me in return
It is you whom my feelings towards are of concern

It is you I don't want to lose
And it is you that's caused me to be confused

It is you who make me feel better then ever
It is you who shows me that happiness is too far

It is you who has brought me all this pain
It is you for whom my desires are in vain

It is you I want to hear the hard things I want to say
And it is you with whom I will never have the time of day

DISCOMBOBULATED: DIFFERENCES

It is you I couldn't keep from loving if I tried
It is you whom I must slam the door on from where it was once opened wide
And so it is you whose eyes I must look into and say this dreadful good-bye

It is you who make me smile with the words of your speech
It is you my heart wants when your body isn't within reach

It is you who the thought of drives me crazy
It is you who knows exactly how to hold me
And it is you who I need to set my heart free

It is you who holds the match I fear will burn
It is you who will never love me in return
It is you whom my feelings towards are of concern

It is you I don't want to lose
And it is you that's caused me to be confused

It is you who make me feel better then ever
It is you who shows me that happiness is too far

It is you who has brought me all this pain
It is you for whom my desires are in vain

It is you with whom I want to keep my friendship
        And say the hard things I want to say
It is you that is straight, but it is I that am gay

I Ain't Playin'

I have a lot on my plate, but if I do nothing else
In this busy life of mine, today, I will find myself

Throw my hands in the air and shout out loud
I'm a one man's man … and for that, I am proud

I see your eyes staring at me
I hear your voices talking quietly

I don't know what the focus of attention could be
But don't let it provoke you to behave rudely or disrespectfully

I don't expect much for my life—you probably wouldn't understand
All I want is to respect you for who you are and for you to respect me for whom I
am

I won't bow down, stay in the dark, or lock the door—for you I refuse to hide
I will stand up, speak my mind, show my colors, be true to myself—for me and
my people, I will show my pride

COMMANDMENT

FYI: Know that I am NOT to be ignored, because when I am bored, you will be floored.

>   Now …

I don't have time for your shit. This is it. Brace yourself; <u>this</u> is how I hit.

How in the hell can you call me baby
When in the past I wasn't your kind to go steady
>   Not the flavor to your gravy or the one for you to love socially or emotionally

Why can't you seem to understand you're not my type of man? I won't be in your plan to deceive the girl in your life with whom you hope to conceive.

Don't sit and think you can play me for a fool, cause I don't feel for you and I'm not gonna be your garden tool. Don't try to hate on me, and I don't appreciate how you call me baby.

I was never the one you wanted to speak to, but now I am suppose to be the one to feed your curiosity by doing things with and to you?

I would try to make this have sense, but you're trying to dirty another's innocence, so why bother—you're just a little boy hiding the truth from himself, his mother, and his father.

I can't believe you came begging me to surrender to your sexuality secrecy. When you have one who holds your heart and treasures your every step—completely.

I suggest you go to her to satisfy your needs, cause I'm not the guy for you to walk over and hump on as you please.

Don't sit and think you can play me for a fool, cause I don't feel for you and I'm not gonna be your garden tool. Don't try to hate on me, and I don't appreciate how you call me baby.

Your secret double-sided life is lame, and I won't be playing in your game—you may not realize it, but things aren't the same. So be nice and think twice before you come back knocking on my doors trying to get me to drop my drawers. I might tell you to 'take a hike' or 'up yours' … butt, isn't that what you want anyway?

In case you missed something, here's a recap: I am not the kind to swing around; I won't lay down, go down, or be down.
No jacket, no shirt, no shoes, no hat … No me, can't you see?

You can't tease me, please me, touch me, or love me—you can't do anything for me
You know, I thought this was going to be hard, but it's actually quite easy.

And by the way, don't call me, baby.

HYPNOTIZED

From the moment I looked at you and you looked at me
My life's been turned upside down, and I've been acting krazy.

You've clouded my thoughts
You're in every word I speak
You're in everything I do
In my heart there isn't room for anyone else, baby; Just you.

You rode me like the hag and are turning me the hell out
Neither you nor I can understand what these emotions and feelings are about

Signed. Sealed. It's over and done—there ain't no goin' back
Officially stamped: I long for YOU. There's no "this," and damn sure ain't no "that."

It's not until this moment—in your arms; thinking about our lives, that I realize
It's by Our Love, that I've been hypnotized.

YOUR.... MY.... OUR....

I need to feel your love in me
I need to feel my love in you
I need to feel our love in each other

I need to feel your hands, your lips
I need to feel you feel my touch, my kiss
I need to feel our love, our bliss

I need to hear your name from my mouth
I need to hear my name from yours
I need to hear our love for each other

I want to know the feel of your breath against my skin,
The sweetness from your kiss, your heat, and your sweat
I need to know you trust in me, and I trust in you.
I need to know we trust each other.

I need to know how your body feels when I hold you tight
I need to know how we'll look together on a snowy, winter night

I need to know how I make you feel
I need to know how you make me feel
I need to know how we make each other feel
I need to know what we feel is real

I fien to know you're going to love me like I love you
I long to know how we're going to love each other

Before I can know these things about you, I need to know you, and before I can
know you, I need to meet you
I can only hope you want to come into my life, like I want to come into yours.
I guess I have to wait until we come into the lives of each other: your ... my ...
our.

Ravish each other....
Devour.

ALONE

To be in a relationship with someone who's:
 Never there for you
 Never spends time with you
 Never shows love for you
But always says to you, "there's no one else in this world for me,"
 And expects you to believe these arid excuses that's simply
 A lame attempt to conceal their infidelity

Finding joy in looking at the falling rain
For it is the only time you can think and breathe without acknowledging your heart's pain

You are alone when you have trouble falling asleep at night in your own bed
 You toss; you turn; and you can't find a comfortable
 Spot on your Down Pillow to rest your head.

Having trouble awakening to start the day
Begrudgingly, you open your eyes
Only to realize … no one beside you lay

When you are full of emptiness and overflowing with depression.
You don't have the strength or energy to do anything but This. And you politically-correctify it and call it creativity. When in actuality, it's a denial-prescription for your personally-prescribed form of self-improvement and creative therapy.
To fill the void of that someone whose eyes you aren't able to look into and see that comfortingly, familiar facial expression.

Too many nights to contemplate the thought that I may have to forever live alone
When I should be living for the moment—for me and myself; Live on My own!

Success: professional and social. All the happy moments to share
Imagine the possibilities to capture the love, the romance, the picturesque moments
They could be endless ... if only there was someone there

WASTING TIME

I need you to come rescue me …

Standing. Staring. Looking
    At the world through my window

Deep in thought wanting to know in life is it
    The cars?
        The people walking?
           Or the dogs barking?
That's passing me by.…
    Or is it life itself?

Seconds are slipping by and confusion is clouding my mind
I still haven't come to a conclusion; no actions have I taken
I spend all my time thinking about my future and what I'll find

Every breath I breathe
Every thought I think
Every site I see
    Saddens me;
For it was a step I didn't take
    Towards an opportunity to have said something I wanted to say;
To have done something I wanted to do …
To have become something I wanted to be.

… to have found the answer to what is preventing me from being free …

The glass is my barrier, but its transparency allows me to see down the street
I still don't know my destination
    Where I want to be
        Or how to get there
But I desire to make the journey on my own with my two feet

… I'm starting to get next to me

BORED

Ma spirit is diein'
Ain't no otha way ta say yit
And I ain't lyin'

THE ONE

My man—the man I love—has finally come
And like an angel with wings, he descended from above

He has an ambience of peaceful strength and a smile of pure, white light
Being with someone has never satisfied my hunger with such delight

He's the sun, the moon, the stars, and the sky;
He's my breakfast, my brunch, lunch, dinner, and my midnight meal
He's the only one who has ever made me feel this real

My man—the man I love—is the music, melody, and lyrics to my happy song
And when I'm not feeling my best, he gives me relational healing all day long

I am the flutter in His heart; He is the spirit in My soul
Together, we write a love story that will never grow old

I love my man as great as good can get
Neither he nor I will ever forget

He is … The Man, I Love.

I CAN DO THIS

Ok, so, I think I may have done it this time
Venturing into a place where opportunities are endless and the light is lime

Crowded streets and buildings that hover near the skyline
Embracing dreams and a life of my own—it's all mine

Taxi? Subway? Bus? There's always feet-to-concrete
Can anyone point me in the direction of Fifth Ave and 47th Street?

Hmmm. They look familiar; must be a star
I miss my Mommy. I'd go back home, but I've come too far

My energy won't be depleted; I won't be defeated
I refuse to be dissuaded; I vow to not become jaded
I promise never to deliver my letter of resignation
I will achieve my goal; I will reach my destination

LOVE WILL FIND ME SOMEDAY

Gonna stop worrying about the past
Where grass has grown; gonna clear a path
Love will find me someday, and it's gonna last

GOOD ENOUGH?

My looks are not great, but my face is flawless
My height is not tall, but my love is endless
My weight is not perfect, but my heart is full
My hair grows; my skin has color
I have 10 fingers, 10 toes, and my eyes run water
But this is not enough …

I don't know what it is that you want me to give
All I have is my life and the way I live
From the span of my hair to the nails on my toes
  Encircling the depth of my soul,
  Encompassing my natural woes.
  I can't give you societal beauty
The understanding of which no one knows

It is my own imperfections that make me a fine independent
One who can offer affectionate love, deep touches, monogamous respect, the
truthful sweetness in a compliment, and a commitment

Am I not good enough for you?
Am I not good enough to give what I have inside?
  My heart
  My life
  My house
    All opened wide
Good enough to give the things I see in your eyes
Good enough to stop your haunting cries
Am I not good enough to give you all the love you want me to?

FOR NOW

For now, I give you permission to overlook and walk on by
For decrepit and overrated love, my broken heart will not vie
The time will come when you realize the one you walked away from is the one
that's got it going on
But by the time you return to get me
From the spot where you left me
I will be long gone

My look may not be good enough
My body may not be hot enough
But my values and morals shall not be broken
        For they are locked, stuffed, bound, and tough
What others think and rate, I don't give a damn
I only want for you to love and like me for who I am

Older. Wiser. Broader. Better.

END OF STORY

Never, no more, will I let thoughts of you haunt me
The cards have been read; the hand's been dealt—we weren't meant to be

I'm standing in the present, preparing to step into the future; leaving you in the past
The prints from where you walked will no longer have an impression in my yard's grass

I'm tired of thinking "what will it be ...," "if only I had ...," "it could have been...."
This is where my new story begins and our fairytale comes to an end.

FATE

It was a calm and sunny day
I was walking down the street, trying to get from Point A to Point B
A chill hit my spine, when I saw you peepin' me
I took you in my eyes and then I prophesized we would never say goodbye
You captured me; I couldn't speak and could barely move my feet
Lookin' back at that day, I now realize it was you I was meant to meet
Floating hand-in-hand as we walked, so much was shared; yet, the First Word we
never talked

EXEUNT FLOURISH

The story still stars you, but features nobody
You weren't the right one to share the stage with me
You aren't the right one to star opposite me
The lights are out around the marquee
And I no longer believe in us, baby

(Honey, this show is over now)

I played the fool in all the drama you put me through
Never knowing what to say or what to do
Cause I believed in me and you

(The time has come; I need a change of scene
This time around, I'm saying what I mean)

I've had it up to here
Not one word more I want to hear; I believed in us
Both you and I
But everything you said was a lie
Now speak the truth, baby; say goodbye

I've had enough of this foolish act
You broke my heart, Love, and that's a fact (mmm, hmmm)

You set the scene and you painted the set
Another audition that I'll forever regret
I refuse to read the lines you wrote in this script
Your contract's up and it's time to recast
This show is over; I'm placing you in my past

Take one last look at me, cause I'm never coming back
This is your final, five-second fade to black

From your deceitful tactics, I've become stronger
I've improved my skills, and emotionally I've grown
Now I don't have to deal with you any longer

Begin collecting your props, cause you're about to go on alone
I've delivered my last line, and I'm about to go
Just pray this monkey don't stop your show

Today's the day I shine in the spotlight
(Make my move; make it real tight)
I'll take my bow and exit Stage Right

A NEW LIGHT BLUES

I'm glad you gon'
Cause to make my life miserable
I can do the damn thing on my own
I don't need you teachin', educatin', and belittlin' me
Got me walkin', talkin', and lookin', like a fool
I'm too damn old for school
I ain't tryin'a be mean
But your *food* was nasty
And your *playtime* was short
Before you know it …
Ooops … engine done out of steam
And ain't nothin' you can preach to me that I ain't already learned
Though if I had paid 'tention
Maybe I wouldn'ta kept comin' back to your triflin' ass just to keep gettin'
burned
No good, ass-kissin', jive-talkin' turkey
This here is my life, and I'm gon live the bitch for me
I don't need you to tell me how special I am
I'm the mountain high; valley low
And the river dam
That keeps the water from lettin' go
I can be the eye of a hurricane
Or the comfort of rain during an afternoon shower
Serene, like the quality of an undisturbed hour
But try the shit again, and I'll show you the right way to go insane
And don't you come back here with no sweet talk
Whisperin' those Sunday words on a Saturday night dance floor
Ain't nothin' you can say that Marvin ain't sung before

THEY THOUGHT WRONG

They thought I loved you,
      But they thought it for no reason
For the love you give is never in season
And if there was something in existence,
      We both know it could never be true

They thought I loved you;
      They're on the outside looking in
How could I love you when I wouldn't
      Know where to begin

My biggest fear is that I could,
      But my love for you would never end
They thought I loved you,
      But never thought you loved me too

How could I love you
      When it's such a crazy thing to do
How could I love you
      When I'm afraid of being next to you
How could I love you
      When I would never be loved by you

I couldn't because it wouldn't be easy
      the way lovin' you is supposed to be;
Where the love I give to you
      resembles the love you give to me

THREE VOICES OF A STORY

I wrote the lyrics for this melody, and today the music is coming from within me

The sun is out and the weather feels right
But I won't see you 'til midnight

Arriving 13 minutes after you
Careful & Cautious, so no one sees the things we do
… looking both ways; checking for stares …

I've been sitting; staring, out my window all day long
This little bird is tired of singing a shadow-love song

It's my heart you're breakin' and your liein' I ain't takin'
If you think I'm going to give you my all, you're mistaken
Three years I've been yearning for you
Three years I've been learning from you …
     Your touches
     Your kisses
     Your feelings …
         … aren't burning

I want it to be just us—both you and me
'Cause I love you without limits—relentlessly.
     Endlessly.

The joy I give and the pain I bring have no boundaries
I can warm your soul, all over and within; play with your emotions, from beginning to end; and fulfill your fantasies, until I hear you sing "Hallelujah! Amen."

ALL I WANT FOR CHRISTMAS

Chestnuts roasting; jack-frost nipping
Snow is glistening; and no one's below the mistletoe
Santa, baby, there's something you must know

You're coming to town
So here's how it needs to go down …
I haven't been naughty—I've been *real* nice
I made my list and I've checked it three times; twice

I don't want much this year—
Just to share my gift with what's on my list—
The one thing I hold dear

I want to build snowmen
Sing a love song
Deck the halls with magic that's a lifetime long
And unwrap a gift that's greater than I can imagine

Cookies and milk will be on the table
The stockings will be hung with care
Santa, if you're willing and able
In the morning, beneath my tree
Something made just for me—
Bold. Strong. Intelligent.
And at least six foot three
In a big, red bow—will be waiting there

On a silent night, while we build desire
Outside, carols will be sung by the choir
Inside, the two of us, kissing by the fire

Bring me a Love that I can have and hold near
To live a wonderful life and ring in a Happy New Year!

St. Nick, I hope you understand
All I want for Christmas is a real good man

TO WENDY; LUV, WHITNEY

I'm real, but you don't need to peep
I'm not shallow like you, baby, and I can go deep

You gon talk about me when my back turns around
So, you better step real hard and fight to win
Cause like shit, I'll hit the ceilin' and you won't knock me down
Move away; get your feet to walkin'
And listen to the words your lips are talkin'

You're not going to kick my behind
You haven't before and it's not going to be different this time
I may be a diva; but I'll meet you in the street
I'll whip you here, there, and everywhere; wherever we meet
Be blacker than coffee with no cream; and give you two lumps to make it sweet
I can shake it fast and drop it on the spot
Just to show you what all I got
So, don't even think you gon stress me
I'll have you dialin' 411 for a 911 emergency

We've talked about all this before
I don't wanna have to tell you anymore
I don't have time for your silly little games; that's all I'm saying
I'm not a child; and with you, I ain' playing
I'm not being mean; I'm being straight-up nice
Don't be a fool, and don't jump on thin ice

What Tomorrow May Bring

We walked by each other; three times each week
Same time. Same Place.
Not once did we speak
Still, on the day we met, you didn't know my face
But your smile crystallized when you recognized my eyes

REVIVIFICATION

Should I be here?

I'll go through with it—to see what I can earn

Curtain's up; Spot is on
        I'm standing Center Stage
All eyes on me

My printed name is on my Birth Certificate
        The original marquee
The empty blank space?
        My age

It's been a while since my talents have filled this place …
        Better smile.
I know they are trying to understand the uncertainty upon my face

I'm just another One:
        jumping around, agreeing, acknowledging, reaffirming—
            pretending to be happy

Looking in front of me, everything seems so bright
        So innocent.… So pure.… So white

Anger burns within me
The gels are amber, but my face is red
Gotta be the product of each light

Sending my message:
        Body movements and voice diction that penetrate the Fourth Wall
Pulse races and lips part as I begin my monologue

They better be ready—this is my return

BETWEEN A HEARTACHE AND A HARD PLACE

A storm full of pain
A relationship filled with rain
I can't stand to lose you, but with you I have nothing to gain

How Can I Want What You Won't Give

I want you here with me
My body—
  gripped, caressed, covered—
By your hands ... a journey

Gently and passionately
Gritty, yet romantically
Nourishingly ... erotically

I must be crazy sitting here wasting my time
Wishing for this love of an amazing kind
It makes no sense—like a lyric poem without reason or rhyme

I want to hold you in my arms while we look into each other's eyes
Your stare, hugging my heart
My smile, shining when you speak

  A voice so powerful and so strong
   So sensuously sweet

I tire of sitting here alone
I reach to pick up the phone
My heart's on the line—apparently you're not home
I can see your phone—sitting, ringing on the shelf
How can I be loving someone, who's loving someone else?

MONSTER'S BALL

I want to feel your body next to me—
     touching me
     trapping me
Your temperature—warming me
Your mouth and tongue—tasting me, teasing me
Your heart and soul—controlling me
Your lips and finger tips—exploring me
Your arms
Your strength—
     protecting me
I want you to use me, tempt me, satisfy and sex me

Love me ... outrageously.

TRICK OR TREAT

I step on behind him; he places his back against the wall
His stare explores my body; he's gorgeous—not too short, not too tall

Not much happens before the bell dings and the doors open
I step off into the journey I was destined to begin

The room is filled with moonlight
This moment feels right
  My body's taken over
And it's been less than five minutes since we met
  This Tuesday in October

I place myself in front of his face
  His eyes are filled with hesitation
To alleviate the pain, he fills our space with casual conversation

My vision is taken with the way he looks
My table is filled with things like his Mama cooks

Why won't he taste my goods?
  Am I not the flavor of milk he drinks?
My body's ready for the sins I know his mind thinks

Takes me by the hand
Leads me like my First Lover
Turns back the bed
  Strips the sheets
    We don't need any cover!

EXPRESS MAIL

Awakening with arms wrapped around me; heavenly.
Feeling him ease out of bed after his muscles fill with tension from hearing the
doorbell ring; frightening.
My love leads me to the kitchen after him, where my eyes see his lips on hers.
"Rain, sleet, or snow. Both of you ... out!"
Reality replaces doubt
My mind; My lips
Both at a loss for words

I CAN ONLY GIVE ALL I HAVE

It's not right for you to love me
It's not good for you to care
I can never be who you want
You could never be what I need
Just say goodbye; don't ask me why
Tomorrow doesn't exist for you and I

The sky will be clearer
The grass will be greener
A weight will have lifted inside
And our spirits will be freer

INDIVIDUALITY

You be you
I'll be me, too

PAID IN FULL

You don't owe me nothing
No apology; no sympathy
It was silly to give myself completely
Because I thought you wanted me

You don't owe me restitution
There was never a contract with you
So don't worry about a resolution
We never said any definite words
We aren't exclusive; thus it's conclusive,
We have no commitment
You are free to do as you choose
It's my own fault; my resentment
I'm the reason I sing the blues

Don't feel sorry, baby
Don't cry, don't think, get your sleep
You don't have to care about me

But now I know I must go on
Something I never had, now is gone
I feel low and empty inside
But I have to uphold my self-respect, dignity, and my pride

I gave you what I had; all my love
Too much, by that one thing
But you don't have to worry,
Cause you don't owe me a thing

I made a fool of me by myself
I never thought there could be someone else
I hope they give you all I gave
And tend to you when you're sick in bed

The words you spoke were nice
The love we made was great

Now I know to think twice
Before I love again—make the same mistake

I shouldn't have wasted my time
Reading between the lines
Thinking something different it would say
When you wrote the story
And it ends another way

Keep your 'best of' wishes
Sugar-coated in niceness
They're still your disses

You don't owe me nothin'
I was the fool
To believe love couldn't be so cruel

You don't owe me ...
No explanation
No restitution or resolution
No sympathy; no empathy
You don't owe me anything, baby ...
I did wrong

INQUIRY

You stepped to the plate; wanted a taste of something new
Liked the quality; loved the style; hooked on a forbidden pleasure
Without a clue of what to do

You wanted to give me everything
Instead, you only delivered broken promises
You have the finances and assets—so you say
But you can't afford This; tomorrow or today

You played me; I was a piece in your game
Claimed to be different from the others, but you're just the same
When you can't stand the heat, you run out the kitchen
I'm done with your disappearing acts; this is where I start my bitchin'

Tell me what happened. Why aren't you here?
With your tail between your legs, you ran like a dog in fear
You said you loved me—past tense; I should have known
In your heart, has hesitancy and hatred grown?

You could never wait to connect, talk with me—always wanted more
Now, you block my emails; won't open the door; my calls you ignore
Your silence is golden—filled with things you've never hinted before
Thankfully, I never slept with you … I'm not your whore

That Day was to be filled with fun and satisfaction
You chose not to show—an unexpected, unplanned, unappreciated action
Then I knew things had changed
Everything once perfect; now seemed strange

Love. A private island. The perfect life together; forever.
You wanted me for me. Maybe it was all a lie
We were to be honest … what happened?
And why?

… now I wash my hands.

WHAT IT'S ALL ABOUT

all i have is respect for myself
and not giving a fuck about anybody else
what they say, think, or do
concern for others is good.
true.
but dignity is better
all about me is the way it's going to be
putting One first, through all types of weather
First Class; Top Priority.

UNDONE

I never knew
Love could be like this
'Never too much' had a limit
And you could do the ills you do

Our love was hard and strong—down to the wire
We were like hot air—we rose higher
We left a mark; scorched on touch—we seared like fire
Picture of perfection; epitome of happiness—we inspired to aspire

Others were looking—getting jealous; envious
Our love has split; there's a rift between us

I never dreamt of the day when I'd close the door in your face and dare you to enter
Cursing you and praying for the pain to be taken away from me
While standing in a phone booth dialing down the center

My friends always told me you would come; then you had to go act a fool
If you never meant to hurt me, then you never would've been so cruel

Don't get it distorted; don't be confused
I'm not into being used or abused

Why couldn't it have been so obvious
That you could be so devious
Now I stand picking the scab off the wound
Why couldn't the real you have been revealed too soon
You should've told me, I would've been more concerned
Protecting myself from your hurt; your fire ... your burn

INFUSION ... CAN YOU FEEL ME?

Lay your head upon my chest
    Heal my heart
    Let your energy run through me
Place your lips on mine
    Kiss me softly
    Let your tongue warm me
Put your hands on me
    Touch, tease me
    Please, please me
Look at me; let the power in your eyes hypnotize me
    Your body supports me
    Your heat relaxes me
    Your scent ... my aromatherapy
I've never felt like this—all day
    Used.
    Dirty.
    Violated.
In a good way!

OPERATION T-8: MORSE CODE

The words you speak, say "yes"
The things you do, say "no"
Get it right, cause I'm about to let you know ...
"You can go."

MOTTO

What I came to get; I got.
What I would like; I've stated and I'll get.
Anything beyond that ...
Respect.

THE MOMENT IN TIME

All I want is to love you
        If only for one minute
                One hour; one year ...
But forever will do

'Til I'm tired and my energy's spent
I'm gon fight for my moment
The instant you take me as I am—
My flaws; my all; the big and the small

Straight through one night
I want you to hold me right; hold me tight

Keep holding strong
'Til I know you belong
You may not know it,
But you will love me someday
And nothing's gonna stand in the way

This is my song
And I'll sing it 'til the break of dawn
I'll be a snow blizzard and a thunderstorm
'Til the spot in my bed is warm

I was made for you
You'll realize it, if it's the last thing I do

My love will shine
For the moment when we're walking; hands intertwined
And realize: I am yours and you are mine

... BUT NOW I SEE

Your actions speak louder than your words
They're saying things from you I've never heard
Outside:
The wind is blowing
The rain is falling
Thunder's rolling and visibility is unclear
But I finally know the things you've wanted me to hear
      Phone calls unreturned.
      Emails unreplied.
      Love unsatisfied.
It took me a while, but now I realize
You never wanted a relationship with me
And there I was: Blind as dumb could be

REWRITE

Looking out into the audience
Millions, but there's no one to please
I'm staring with an uncomfortable ease
Standing on stage; my story being told by the piano's keys
This is a tune I've cried before
The music must stop; I'm not gon' sing it anymore
This song is overdone
I need a piece about me; a signature one
I need something new
A duet that's true
With someone who cradles me closely, like a mic in a stand
To whisper to me softly
Talk to me slowly
To swoop and croon every note
Sensuously … seductively
Someone to be the ink in my lyric pen
The bridge that connects the new with the then
Repeated with a catchy refrain
That reflects joy and pain
A melody to serenade all ears
A portrait of words that captures our future years …
Alleviates our love fears …
Paints our romance in tears
And sung by a sultry voice that brings water to our eyes
And loud enough to quiet our endearing sighs

MOMENT OF TRUTH

When I came home from work the other day
The look on your face told me
Someone was taking my place
It broke my heart deeply
To know we'd end this way
Your love was like a promise
A promise that you'd never keep
So how can I forgive you
When … only you could treat me like this

It's hard for me to comprehend
Why you want our love to end
You said you'd always love thee
And that we would be together
Today we're having some real good weather
Fly, My Love. This is the day that I set you free

COME TO ME (BABY)

i've saved it, now i'll give it all to you
[come on babe, i'll give it to you]
you have to do it right
[come on babe, do me right]
or i'm gon' tell you what to do
[come on babe, i'll do it for you]
give it to me, make me go oooh
'cause this is the night
[come with me; this is the night]

come hold me baby, i need some tender care
come here babe, and take me there
come on babe, enjoy this special place
just come baby, i'll put a smile on your face

i'll treat you nice
better than you can dream
i'll go slow and let you see what i mean
enjoy it all; make you scream

THE REMIX

The rules have changed
This time I'm taking charge
So save your bullshit; I can't be charmed

S-O-S

No longer striving for perfection
Nor being driven by greed
But there's still a lot that I need
Too many times have I been burned
And not once did I learn
To put myself before another's concern
Now the tables have turned; I want desperately—
My emotional health is in jeopardy—
For someone to come along and set me free
To release the struggles that burden me
Like air that's lifted from my chest
I want to float and worry less
Be my angel
Put my soul at ease
Rescue me ...
Love me ...
... Please

I Don't Think So

No time, No more
Bless me for thy hath not been bothered
No time to sit around, count the days
Trying to figure out how many children you've fathered
No more ... Not I
No time to let you flaunt your lovers in my face
No more will I let you come late just to play in my space
I desire attention; I require high maintenance
But to tolerate your B.S., I could never have enough patience
No time to sit around and stress over competition
No more ... Not I
My design's original; my quality's good
I guarantee satisfaction!

RESUSCITATED

I got a new life
This time I'm free
I'm gon smell the flowers
And take care of me
I'm done taking your pain
I don't like you enough to go insane
Today's a new day, and I'm starting right here
The first step I take is not to live in fear
This is the time I love me for me
A day of peace and joy … my kind of therapy

WHAT DO BROKEN HEARTS KNOW

You don't want me now
But one day you did and another day you will
I'll show you, somehow
I ain' lookin' for a second chance
I ain' lookin' for a new romance
All I really need
All I really want
All I gotta know …
If someone loves you, will they always
I want you to tell me so
Since you used to love me, but don't nowadays
I'm the one you disrespected and treated with disgrace
The recurring dream you've tried to displace
You think you've thought the last of me
When you ain' seen nothing yet
I may be easy to get over
But you will never forget

SPEAK

All I wanted was to love you
But I guess that's too much
You've never called my name
And I've never felt your touch
There's a pain in my heart that shouldn't exist
We're always someplace between 'broken up' and 'back together'
What kind of relationship is this?
With no idea of what I'm facin'
This confusion is killing my concentration
My strength is gone
My love's worn; my heart's torn
I'm tired of waiting for you
  From late at night thru the early morn
If there is someone else
  Just tell me who
Don't be afraid of what I'll do
  Or the actions I'll take
There's only our future at stake

PARAMOUNT

I melt with the touch of your skin
Our bodies intertwined—no beginning or end
Overwhelming pleasure as you press into me
Harmonious joy; ecstatic ecstasy
Filled with fear from our first sight
Everything thus far has been so wrong
This can't possibly be right
You invaded my world with the warmth of your eyes
You captured my soul with your insatiable stares and seductive sighs
I fall for you each time we speak
Yet when I wake, your face I never see
You rise to leave before sunrise
Too weak to look me in the eyes
The water signals irrepressible cries
The only words spoken: Just go, I'm gonna be alright
My actions, I should regret
Others will despise—because they wouldn't dare
But, I'm happy:
        You fulfilled my need
        You satisfied my greed
One could never live a moment like this;
Only read
To this refreshing feeling …
To this exhilarating experience …
Nothing can compare

YOUR EVERYTHING

I give myself to you as I set myself free
You drive me wild with your body
And your eyes; and your presence
And with every move you make
With each kiss you take
You're establishing precedence
I've never known a touch like yours
A touch my body longs to recognize
It's like wandering, lost in a forest
While wondering ... could I really be living this?

IMPOSSIBLE OATH

You were to be my morning ray of sun
My evening moon
And my midnight desire
Guaranteed to give more love than I could have ever expected
Declared to be unlike any other my heart's ever detected
In cultured tongues you pledged to make me speak
If I looked in your eyes, you said my knees would get weak
Vowed to protect me when I'm meek
And understand me when I'm wrong
Claimed to be brave enough to love me
Strong enough to care, completely
And swore to never leave me

I was a fool to believe all your lies
Now I'm sad, but I'm also wise
This wasn't suppose to happen to me
I am an example
Someone others strive to be
All I wanted was someone with whom I could grow and live
Apparently asking for something you didn't want to give
I'll say goodbye, so don't piss me off
And don't make my roots show
I'll drop all the knowledge
You don't know
Because like a stage I went through
I am soooooo over you

POETRY 4 PLAY

Your voice whispering in my ear
Your words dripping down my neck
Your hands roaming my body
Your desire building my internal fire
Our limbs twist
Our bodies turn
We each feel it:
    The intensity
    The passion
    The heat
    The burn
Our lives defined in the moment we could never resist

COMING TO

Your love is like crack
And your crack is whack
Had me going out of my mind
Looking like a fool
Thinking that you love me
When you don't feel like I do
I'm not an addict; I don't hallucinate
You are my biggest mistake
Let's get THAT straight
Next time around, what I see will be real
And what I feel …
It will be ideal

VACANCY

Words unspoken.
Feelings unexpressed or expressed without emotion.
The doors that are left unopened
Of all the things I never told ya
I have to say "Goodbye, baby."
I need closure.

AN INSTANCE

Let's wait....
Let's have a moment
This is a time ...
A time when I can never find the right rhyme
Or that perfect line ...
The way to say what's on my mind
In my life, I am thankful to have you
For whom you are and the things you do
Today, I am lucky.
But forever and always,
I am blessed ... gracefully; gratefully

MYSTERY SOLVED

I'm mad because I love you and you know that, too
Yet, I failed to see that for me you didn't care
And what I have you could get anywhere
It's not much, but to me it's special
Who knew giving it, could be so regretful
I believed what I wanted
Felt what I needed
Desired for you to hold me
When you pledged to protect me in your arms
Silly, how I fell for your promises, your lies, and your charms
I'm leaving you; closing the book
CASE CLOSED!
It's all that I can do

MAY'S FLOWERS

The morning started out dark and dreary
Clouds moving into each other's way
The air—wet & misty; a shadowed gray
It was forecasted as a light shower
We ... no one ... expected a downpour
Somehow, I was able to make out the horizon, clearly
While washing away the pain
All it took? A walk in the rain

DON'T BOTHER ME

The pain you bring, I don't deserve
Not gon let anything work my nerve
Don't wanna be bothered
Don't care what your mama say
Don't wanna talk to your friends
Who cares what they think, anyway
I'm not in the mood
Just wanna be left alone
Pack your shit and be gone
I'll do my thing, on my own

A STRANGER TO LOVE

The love I give to you
Makes you uncomfortable
Many days it's like we've never met
I'll sit and stare
Tell myself, "I don't care"
Each Anniversary, you're long gone
Yet, I'll sit and wait there, all alone
In the beginning it seemed strange
But now, it's obvious, you'll never change
I know you want me to leave
But I refuse to let our love die
I'm not ready.... I won't grieve
To get your feelings realigned
I'll do everything I can try

MORE THAN THE USUAL

I need something more than the usual.
Someone unusual.
Something special with an unusual someone.
Someone with that special, unusual something.

Someone who ...
... Understands and accepts me for who I am—my flaws and all
... Knows when to be strong and stronger; yet, has moments of weakness
... Is loving and loveable
... Realizes that looks are important, but are not everything
... Knows that a brain that's used is beautiful
especially when accompanied by a personality
... Is an outsider but also enjoys being an insider,
... Likes to do crazy things just because it's possible—rather the activity makes
sense or not.
... Has a sense of self, a sense of humor, and a sense of self-respect.

All I want is something and someone true. Is that someone you?

IM 2 IM: THE LAST MESSAGE

Contradiction1881: You there?

Contradiction1881: What won't I believe-what do you have to tell me?

QueSeraSera: I say this cause I dare: You're fired; I'm letting you go, baby.

Contradiction1881: You like me.

Contradiction1881: I love you

Contradiction1881: I suspect you feel as I do

Contradiction1881: I always know you are gonna be there

Contradiction1881: Just like you know I will be too

Contradiction1881: We can't get past this online game

Contradiction1881: But the feelings are there

QueSeraSera: They're not the same

QueSeraSera: Not the way they used to be

Contradiction1881: I was building a palace for us. I knew that soon you'd come to me

Contradiction1881: I knew it like I know my name

Contradiction1881: But, I've lost it; I've lost you

Contradiction1881: It's gone; You're gone

Contradiction1881: And so are my dreams … washed away by the sea

Contradiction1881: So think about what I lost; what we lost

QueSeraSera: I'm done

Contradiction1881: Don't criticize

Contradiction1881: Don't chastise

Contradiction1881: Come wipe my tears

QueSeraSera: Stop the poetry.

QueSeraSera: I don't want to hear it; there's no need for crying eyes.

QueSeraSera: I'm done.

QueSeraSera: It's not worth it anymore:

QueSeraSera: Put your feet to the floor; use the door

QueSeraSera: The words you speak no longer make me weak.

QueSeraSera: You think you care for me, but you don't

QueSeraSera: I would've worshipped you; but now, I won't.

Contradiction1881: Tell me how wrong I was

QueSeraSera: You're never wrong for going after what you want

Contradiction1881: So why the fight? Why tonight?

QueSeraSera: I need to know where I stand:

QueSeraSera: In your mind?

QueSeraSera: Your thoughts?
Contradiction1881: In my heart.
QueSeraSera: Am I still your ultimate wish?
QueSeraSera: Am I the source of your bliss?
Contradiction1881: I want to start fresh
Contradiction1881: Sweep away the dirt
QueSeraSera: Like I've already said
QueSeraSera: I love hard, but I don't hurt
QueSeraSera: I need love, too. My heart is itchin'
QueSeraSera: But I don't have time for fiction
Contradiction1881: So, please, play with me
Contradiction1881: Stay with me
Contradiction1881: Don't ever leave me!
QueSeraSera: Stop burning my energy!
QueSeraSera: If you love me; want to love me
QueSeraSera: Give me something real—something I can feel
QueSeraSera: If you're not afraid
QueSeraSera: So?
Contradiction1881: If it ends like this, we end
QueSeraSera: Forever
Contradiction1881: I won't be back
QueSeraSera: You don't even know my name.
QueSeraSera: We have yet to begin.

THOMAS GREGORY

I didn't enjoy the way you loved me

Your imprint; My scar
A welt.
When I see it and glide my fingertips across it
I think back on how I felt

The instant I first saw you—my life was changed
From that point, things would never be the same
The moment we allowed our eyes to meet
I was swept away by an undercurrent that knocked me off my feet
I opened my heart; my soul; my arms; my eyes
Waited for your love to flood into thee
From the valley low beyond the highest mountain peak
I aimed to be the river you would seek
I laugh, because it seems so strange
But I now know, to never love one who's Primary and Sur are both a First name

The power you had over me laid in …
Your strength; your grip; your hold
Once, I was strong; you made me weak
Manipulated; seven days per week
I was never to be controlled
It's been seven years, and about you, I still can't speak
Yet, you are still the freedom I seek
Your thoughts and scent are still fresh
Sometimes you're the thing that comes over me
Barring you from being a distant memory

When we separated, I was scared
Didn't know how I would face life on my own
Met many since then and not one could be compared
Thanks to you, I'm still alone …

And waiting for someone to love me—
The way I deserve to be

LoVe In LiMbO

just because the sex is tight
it doesn't make your cheating all right
your love is mine; like mine is yours
and that's just how things should be

not saying that you belong to me
cause, babe, shackles and chains are crazy
we had ... honesty ... monogamy
words that don't exist to many
we have to rectify
and survive to testify
your heart is mine; like mine is yours
and that's just how things should be
no more blaming you; blaming me ... baby
we gotta work it out; discover what it's all about
in the beginning, we were winning
then temptation brought the situation
i've been praying all year
cause losin' you is my biggest fear
your love is mine; like mine is yours
and that's just how things should be

what made you want to act disrespectfully
we have to get this right
and put it all behind us; out of sight
what's it all about ... let's work it out

blow my body
like you blow my mind
come back to me baby
i may let you slide ... this time
your love is mine; like mine is yours
and that's how things have to be

FOOL'S PARADISE

Candlelit dinners with instrumental melodies in the air
Relaxing in bed, being seduced by that seductive stare
Looking in your eyes and smiling from ear to ear
Waking each day with no hurt or fear
You used to make me feel like I could shine
And every second that you breathed was Mine
Showered me with roses and butterfly kisses
Now, I can't describe exactly what This is

I don't know you; you've become a stranger
I can't let you put my life or my heart in danger
I'm tired of your lies
And sick of the late-night cries
Instead of joy, you bring me pain
Give me peace before I go insane
And swear in vain

I can do bad all on my own
Your love no longer keeps me warm
I speak the words parked on my tongue's tip …
Don't think about me; don't hit me on my hip
There's the door.
Jar the floor.
Baby, I don't want you no more

PUSSYFOOTING

I'm not one of your leeches
So I'll spare you the speeches
Listen to me … Give in to me
Baby, I need This

Your motions are still
Your words are quiet
How am I to know your heart's will
If you won't say it or display it?

It's not illegal, but playing with my heart is a crime
Will I be yours? Will you be mine?
No pressure; take your time
Just please, make up your mind

The answer is simple—just "yes" or "no"
Say the word, so I'll know:
If I should stay
Versus
If I should go

Or, are you just another Fly-By-Night Romeo?

IT'S A W.RAP

When we started out we both were cool
Now, you've lost your mind and you're acting like a fool
First you raised your voice; then you raised your hand
Apparently you forgot, I don't jump on command

Not gon' stand for a bruise or abrasion
I've had enough of the Devil's invasion
Forget about Mimi, this is my emancipation
I'm getting out of this difficult situation
Flying free ... pleasing me
I'm tired of diein'
This time I'm tryin'
No more cryin'
And I ain't liein'
A miracle's conceived!
See; I believed ...
One day I'd rise above
The pain you gave and called it Love
So many nights I should've thrown your shit outside
Don't know what took me so long to realize
 That you were no damn good to me
 That you were no damn good for me
 That you are just no damn good; from any point I could see
I thought back on good days; wanted them again
When you sang love songs from beginning to end

What we had is too far gone
So I'll pick up my pieces and walk on
I've made up my mind, this time
You broke my heart; THAT'S *your* crime

MY FAULT? HELL NO, IT'S ON YOU.

I never know when you'll attack
Sometimes I'm lonely; sometimes I'm scared
No one's around to have my back
PUNCHING me with closed fists
The pain I feel could never be bliss
SCREAMING 'you work my fucking nerve'
And say what I get, I deserve
Broken rib; displaced jaw; two black eyes that can't stand the light
Thank you; I'm walking around in shades at a half past midnight
PUSHING me against the wall
KICKING me when I'm bleeding and curled in a ball
You THROW me to the floor
YELLING names: bitch, cunt, cum slutt, whore
Followed by 'I love you…. but you're a bore'

Been trying to get you to hear what I've been saying
Now, I'm tired of pleading with you to see I ain' playing
Fighting with you has been no use
I can't sit around and tolerate your abuse
It's one of your crazy notions
If you think I'm gon' let you fuck with my emotions

You don't love me when your feelings turn to hate
And you're obsessive; compulsive
Lost, in that crazed, psychotic state
I'm not the source of your insecurities
And you won't complicate my life with your difficulties
I will no longer bow down to your stupidity or your demands
From this point on, I'm taking a stand and raising my hands
This is where I interrupt your best-laid plans

ME 'N YOU

I know you're leaving me
I can hear it in your lies
Each morning I rise
I can see it in your eyes
It's in the way you walk
When you turn away from me
It's in the way you talk
When you're not around me
Somewhere along the line, something went wrong
My lyrics no longer match your music
This isn't our song
I can feel it in the way you touch me
When you hug, but no longer hold me
It's how you smile, when you're unhappy
It's how you hold your head down
When I come around
It's how I know you don't dream of me
But have nightmares involving me
It's been my past; it's become my destiny
That's how I know …
You've already left me

WHEN WORDS WOULDN'T WORK

You said you'd protect me and keep me warm
Treasure me and never hurt me
You said you'd say goodbye if you chose to leave
You lied; what you did I can't believe
While I was gone you walked out the door
I guess you couldn't say you didn't want me anymore
I thought you were strong; you proved to be weak
Didn't look me in the eyes; weren't brave enough to speak
Did you know that you hurt me?
Did you intend for me to go crazy
I was thinkin' I wasn't good enough
But I was wrong
You knew you didn't belong
You left me hangin' on

Baby, why are you gone?
Why'd you make promises you wouldn't keep
Promises that when broken, would make me weep
What you did ain't right
What didn't you like?
Did I love you too much
Gave love that was a little too hard; a little too tough
You said it was you I could always trust
And we'd always be together
But you didn't stay
Instead you went away
What happened to us?
We haven't had forever

There are times when I sit
Looking out the window
Daring myself to see how long I can stare
Into the quiet night; the open air
One dark, the other bare
Wondering if you ever did care

Waiting for you to come through the door
Baby, will you ever return?

Time continues to slide away
I'm getting better, day by day
Yet, I still feel burned
I'm stronger and now I know
It was all a bunch of bullshit

To me, I never thought you would lie
Or leave, without a whisper of goodbye
Don't you worry; have no fear
Like Mary J., I won't shed a tear
Ain't no cryin' after all your liein'
Don't come back; Don't mistake this for vyin'
Your words were to be free
Open to breathe; honest with me
But that was back then; in the beginning

FOR WHO I AM

Can't hold your hand as we walk down the street
You're afraid to face the stares (you think) we'd meet
Why aren't you strong enough to stand on your two feet?

It's sunny out, but my heart's stone cold
You claim to love me, but the words I've never been told
Once, I was satisfied; but, now it's getting old.

Yet, here I am goin' out my mind
Doin' shit trying to please you
Forgetting myself; leaving me behind
My family doesn't recognize me
Mama's asking, 'What've you done with that child of mine'

It's time for me to be who I truly am
How you feel
Like it or love it
I don't give a damn

I make my own; buy my own
Living my life of luxury
I refuse to be your show piece; will not be your trophy
You're wrong if you think I need you to spend money on me

Allowed you to reach your boiling point; dispense your anxiety
You turn over, forget about me, and I smile like I'm happy
Just to please you
You're wrong if you think being in the bedroom is the only way you can pleasure
me
I don't know who you've done before, but that's not what I get off to

Shut your mouth; don't tell me I'm whining
I'm spilling my needs that will redeem me
Cause what you're pitching; I ain' buying

You might have gotten by with these things before
But this is Me; I require more.

REAL LOVE

I need a real love
It's time I accept reality
Baby, you aren't that in to me
You know I love you
But it's time I love myself and be loved too
I need a love I can feel
A love that's real
Forget the other things you do
How can you ignore me with your touch
And treat me like you do
Maybe I love you too much?
I'm tired of being treated this way
You got my whole life in disarray
Worrying and stressing about a bunch of hype
When I'm not the type that cares what your friends think or say
This light is mine and I'm gon' shine
Each morn I wake will be a new day
I'm too good to be misused
Wednesday through Sunday; I shouldn't be singing Monday's blues
I want someone who loves like I do
I need a real love
Doesn't have to be complete bliss
Just a love that actually exists
I need love
A love that resembles the kind I give
A love that makes me wanna live
A love that makes my heart jump a beat
A love that makes me wanna skip down the street
A love I can feel
A love that's real

SELFISH

i opened my heart to you
bared my soul
shared secrets i've never told
now you're here wasting time
expecting me to read between the lines
and understand what's on your mind
i know you're upset; something went wrong
tell me what happened; what's going on?

you're acting in ways you never have before
i've had it up to here; i can't take it anymore
don't keep it to yourself
confirm my fear
tell me there's someone else

what we had may not have been publicly shown
but in our hearts it was known
we weren't to become scandal
something to be talked about or read
you did like i said
i knew you would; you didn't think you could
i predicted the pain you inflicted
loving you was to be something i could handle
how could you hurt me this way
and more with every word you say
and everything you do
like I saw our demise
sooner or later you'll realize
i have feelings too

WHEN I THINK OF YOU

when i think of you
i think of you leaving me
my heart broke; simply shattered
my world stopped; nothing else mattered
emotional; unstable
completely thrown
a way of life i've never known
when i think of you
i think of you leaving me
allowing me to be happy
you wanted me to fail
never thought i'd win
24/7 i'm content
outside and within
from the break of day
to late night's end
when i think of you
i think of all the pain one person can bring
but now i've found this thing
and ... mmmm ... it makes my heart sing
it's what we could've had
but you wanted to act stupid
too bad; so sad
when i think of you
i think of you leaving me
all alone in an empty space
when i think of you
i think of you leaving me
and allowing someone else to take your place
when i think of you
i think of you leaving me
and the joy and peace i experienced *then*
when i think of you
i think of what i have now and what could have been
when i think of you

i think of you leaving me and i wonder....
would you do it again?

DON'T CRY FOR ME

Don't have fear; don't shed a tear
Don't feel sorry; don't you worry
There's nothing for you to do or say
Things aren't as they appear to be—
      That's your perception; your view of reality
I'm not down; I'm not out; I'm fighting to win and I'm gonna be okay

Don't try to live for me
      This is my life; my view—through the eyes of me
It's designed the way I intend it to be
Don't try to be me
      You're not wearing my shoes; you don't see what I see
My sun shines from the break of day to late night's end
Don't try to understand how I experience things
      For you may never comprehend
Please …
Don't cry for me
When you're on the outside looking in

Stand by me …
Celebrate with me …
Be happy for me.

I Know You Do

Walk on by like you don't see me
    Turn your head; I don't care
Pretend like you don't hear me
    The words I say
Cover your ears; I know you're listening
    And you know I'm still here … and there
    Hell, to you, I'm everywhere
Ignore the thoughts you think of me
    Deep inside, desire is burning ferociously
Live your days like you don't envision life with me
    I know you do
    I have you trippin' out
    I know what it's all about
When you're drifting down the street
    And you see someone …
    You think of me
At night when you're trying to sleep
    Laying in your bed; longing to hold me
    Wanting to be next to me
    I know you think of me
Your hands are wet
    Filled with sweat
    Itching to touch me
Your tongue gliding along my body
Your nose inhaling me
Your mind surrounding me
    Becoming one with me
Open your eyes
    See me here
Uncover your ears
    Hear me clear
Don't keep fooling yourself
Don't keep killing yourself
    Your body's filled with agony
    The pain from denying me
    Stop all the craziness you do

The nonsense you put yourself through
Embrace reality
You want me, don't you?

OPTIONS

Forget about some other
You'll never have another like me
To balance you when you're strong
Correct you when you're wrong
To think we belong

Loved you freely
How could you do this to me?
Broke my heart.
Ripped. Shredded.
Torn apart.

Claimed the years between us were too great
Too large in scope
Too much for you to cope
Your decision
Your mistake
Let's get that straight

Cherished each day
Waking next to you
Looking in your eyes with nothing to say
So I smile, which is all I could do
Except …
Get up
Get dressed
And walk away

PLAYED TO EXHAUSTION

It feels like I'm reliving my past
Where the more I give; the more you take for granted
I'm tired and all burned out
My energy's drained
My patience is spent
I don't think I'm gonna last
I won't fight in this bout
It's time we talked; figured this entire thing out
Besides the tears and fears
I have nothing to show or represent
All I've lost;
All I've gained
From then 'til now—
Somehow …
It's been five years
And I still don't know
What did I do to deserve you?

PROMISE WORDS

I said I loved you
I said we could be together
I said I would have you
        'til death do us part
I expected you to smile and say
        We'll have forever
"There's hate in my heart"
        I heard you say
Then you turn and walk away

Still …

I say I love you
I say we can be together
I say I will have you
        'til death do us part
And I mean it …
        Cross my heart

SPEECHLESS

Speechless.
Choked by a feeling I never knew existed
Thoughts, emotions, and tongue
All jumbled and twisted
I need to fix this

Speechless.
Bound by your kissing me deeply
Breathing new life in to me
Speechless.
Confused by your clouding my mind; intoxicatingly
Spoiling me in ways pampered should never be

Speechless …
Because until I met you, I've always had something to say
From the thoughts I'd think
To the songs I'd sing
And the words I'd write
Anything, just to make it through the day
Then came you, taking my breath and speech away

YOUR STYLE

Some boys think they know all about me
From my childhood history
To solving my inner mysteries
Yet like the Child of Destiny
They just don't know 'bout me

You know just how to treat me
From the way you greet me
To the way you kiss me
Even how you miss me

You know …
I'd give myself, to you, completely
And still want to give you more
'Til you know for sure
The way you do me is so right
Just the way I like

I like …
The way you touch me; the way your eyes call me
The way you do it all; rough, up against the wall
Gently and tenderly, without letting me fall
Playing on the fact: I'm short and you're tall

I like the way you …
Kiss and lick my lips
The way you bump and grind my hips
Validate me; complete me
The way you work your magic on me
Intoxicate me; drive me crazy

I like …
The way you rock me slowly
The way you hold and control me
The way you convince me I'm your one and only
The way you make it worth my while

I like it all, baby
But I love your Initial-Named Style

FAMILY, TO ME

Family, to me, is being all that one can be
Open. Honest. Supported. Driven and free.
A base; a core
The place where love is never out of date
It satisfies; it satiates
Family; you couldn't ask for anything more

Family, to me, is history
A telling of who we are, where we're going,
        and where we've been
Not ones to seek an end
Family is a journey of man
Leaving footprints in the sand
Continuing towards a prosperous destiny
Leaving behind a golden legacy

Family, to me, is about togetherness and beauty
A reflection ...
Of what was
Of what is
Of what will be

Family is ...
You.
Me.
Us.
We.

A fountain of love without question.

LOVE CHESS

Looking into your eyes, I could never say
It hurts to see you standing so far away
I knew I was last on your list
But you gave me more than I've ever known to exist
You never said you loved me until you said goodbye
I was angry and frustrated with myself for loving you
Those were the tears you saw me cry
For 7 months you were all mine
Now you tell me you were lovin' all of mankind
Putting your hands, your lips, your tongue, your dick
In places they didn't belong
Yet you still don't think you cheated on me or did me wrong
I played my part and now you treat me like this
You didn't mean to hurt me?
You didn't think I could bleed?
Forget the red roses; keep your stale candy
Give me my joy and my happiness
It's your pity I don't need

FEEDBACK

Let's lay a foundation
Begin this journey to a new destination
Together we'll transform
Speak our hearts
Listen to our pain
Open our minds
Embrace all we can gain
The things we could never say
The things we ignored each day
This is our platform
I talk to you
You talk to me
Let's discuss how things should be

HOW COULD ...

How could you let me fall for you
Knowing all the pain I'd suffer through
How could you hold me close; whisper what I like to hear
Stroke my heart; erase my fear
How could you welcome me into your atmosphere

How could you hit me with your heart-break words
When I did my best to love you right
I let you in; I lowered my standards
Maybe I did too much and held on too tight

Claimed you weren't ready for it
Couldn't give me what I wanted
Said I deserve more; I should be a chosen-one
How could you bar discussion—have it all said and done

Tell me ... how could you close the door?
Tell me ... how could you quit?
Better yet, tell me ...
How could I be so damn blind ... and so unintelligent???

UNSTABLE

You're an emotional rollercoaster ride
Not built for safety; too wild
You go from wishy-washy to touchy-feely
From being sexy to being creepy
Lacking nonchalance; nothing's ever in stride

My family; my friends—we all think you're insane
Withhold trial; convict me, baby …
I'm guilty
For exposing myself to your pain
Opening my heart; forgetting the rules of the game
Overlooking that all dogs bite the same

Feed me what you want; tell me your lies
Just don't hurt me; don't make me cry

IF I KNEW THEN WHAT I KNOW NOW

If I knew then what I know now
I would've been wiser, stronger, and prepared; somehow
Wise enough to know not to trust the words you speak
Cause you're a man; and like a man ... always weak
Secretly trying to indulge in the pleasure-vices you constantly seek
Strong enough to voice my heart and mind's questions
The one's whose answers would have informed me of your now-known indiscretions
The ones that were then classified as side effects of your depression
I would have been meticulous and concerned enough to be prepared
I would have had a way to handle knowing that about me; you never cared
And to let you in my heart, my life, my bed; I wouldn't have dared
I would have easily opened the doors to let you move on
But I didn't know that I could make it with you gone

If I knew then what I know now
You never would have heard those three words I whispered gently
You never would have caused me to cry uncontrollably
And you never would have underestimated the power of me
But that was yesterday; back when I was blind
When I had my eyes closed and never thought to use my mind
I didn't know then, but I do know now

LIKE I DO

Do you know what it's like …
To have eyes look at you
Without interest or emotion
Devoid of love; not a trace of intensity
To have hands hold you
Without a sense of support or devotion
Lacking protection and the warmth of desire?
I do.

Do you know what it's like …
To love someone
To care for someone
To be with someone
Who doesn't love you
Care for you
Appreciate you
Or want to be with you?
I do.

Do you know what it's like to be with someone to whom you could be anyone?
I do.

It's like …
A flicker of a flame
In an open space
A gust of wind
On a cloudy day
A dream
When you can't sleep
A thought that passes
When you don't have time to think.

Do you know what it's like to be in love with you?
I do. I really do.

Do you know what it's like to be loved by you?
I …

HURT

It hurts
Through and through
I'm confused and I don't know what to do
Along this road no signs lead to you
We've moved on; for me, there haven't been any others
We've been friends, now; longer than we were lovers
There are moments when I want to be your prize
It hurts …
You feel otherwise
When you manage to look at me, I can see it in your eyes
My failure to satisfy; you scrutinize
My attempts to please; you criticize
Nothing is good enough: me or the things I do
Slowly, truth has come into view—
I no longer do it for you
It hurts
When you speak to me, there's something in your voice
It tells me I wasn't, I'm not, and I'll never be your choice
Something more fills your body with tension
Pick up the phone; call me
I'll filter the things I'm not supposed to mention
It hurts
Come closer; don't let it pain you to stand next to me
Relax; let yourself touch my body
Let me be a part of you; an extension
It hurts…. but, what hurts the most:
Knowing that we used to be;
The life I envisioned, I'll never see;
And the one you will love will not be me

CELEBRATING ME

This is me.
This is who I am.
This is me; this is how I feel.
This is me; This is who I am and how I feel.
This is me.
This is all me …
    FOR REAL!

978-0-595-52148-7
0-595-52148-7

Printed in the United States
203036BV00004B/31-81/P